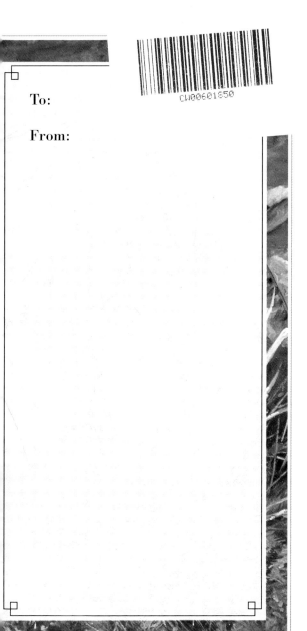

To:

From:

Though now you are bereft and
ways seem black,
With emptiness and gloom on
every hand;
Someday Time's healing touch
will lead you back,
And gradually your heart will
understand

That what you bore must come to
one and all,
And Peace, the clean white
flower born of pain,
Will slowly, surely, rise from
sorrow's pall,
And happiness will come to you again.

MARGARET E. BRUNER

The only courage that matters is the kind that gets you from one moment to the next.

MIGNON MCLAUGHLIN

Have you come to the Red Sea
place in your life
    Where, in spite of all you can do,
There is no way out, there is no
way back,
    There is no other way but
through?

ANNIE JOHNSON FLINT (1866-1932)

This existence of ours is as
transient as autumn clouds.
To watch the birth and
death of beings is like
looking at the movements of
a dance.
A lifetime is a flash of
lightning in the sky.
Rushing by, like a torrent
down a steep mountain.

BUDDHA (c.563-c.483 B.C.)

For the sake of all who love you,
and yourself, learn to step aside
sometimes into a place of silence,
where you can watch the quiet
stars and rediscover peace.

PAM BROWN, b.1928

The mind has a thousand
eyes,
And the heart but one;
Yet the light of a whole life
dies
When love is done.

FRANCIS WILLIAM BOURDILLON

I would like to carry you away to somewhere rich with sunshine and the scent of flowers, somewhere out of the sound of clocks, out of the reach of schedules and telephones, a place where time moves drowsily and the days are full of a quiet contentment. Where for a little while, no one will demand your heart or mind or time. Where hurts can heal, and you can find yourself.

PAM BROWN, b.1928

Out of land made desolate by
fire and flood and war comes new
life – feeding on the past, but
turning to the sun. Out of your
most unhappy heart will come
new joy.

PAM BROWN, b.1928

Love is not changed by
    Death,
And nothing is lost and all
    in the end is harvest.

EDITH SITWELL (1887-1964),
from *Eurydice*

Though they sink through the sea
 they shall rise again;
Though lovers be lost love shall
 not;
And death shall have no
 dominion.

DYLAN THOMAS (1914-1953),
from *And Death Shall Have No Dominion*

They shall not grow old, as we
that are left grow old:
Age shall not weary them nor the
years condemn.
At the going down of the sun, and
in the morning,
We will remember them.

LAURENCE BINYON (1869-1943)